Scaredy Cat

Written by Dee White
Illustrated by Tracie Grimwood

Pippa had lots of pets.

Cass was Pippa's cat.
Cass liked to sleep in the sun.

Spot was Pippa's new dog.

Spot wagged his tail.
"Woof!" he said.

Cass ran up the tree.
"Come down!" said Pippa.

Cass just sat in the tree.
“Meow!” said Cass.

Pippa and Spot stood on a chair.

"Come down, Cass," said Pippa.
"Do not be a scaredy cat.
Spot will not hurt you."

Cass did not come down.
“Woof!” said Spot.

Cass ran down the tree.
She ran and ran.

Cass was scared.
She ran into the fish pond.

Spot and Pippa had to help Cass to get out of the fish pond.

Cass let Spot lick her.
Spot wagged his tail.

After that, Spot and Cass played together ...

... far from the fish pond!